The Bagel Book

The Bagel Book

by June Roth

GROSSET & DUNLAP
A FILMWAYS COMPANY
Publishers • New York

Dear Reader:

What is it about a bagel that makes you smile? Is it the pleasant sound when you say "bagel," or the great taste when you eat it? Could it be the aroma when it's toasting? Perhaps it's the texture when you bite through the shiny crust to the firm bread inside. Is it the knowledge that a bagel is a healthy food made with no additives or preservatives? Maybe it's the bagel's adaptability to be many things to many foods, without losing its own identity.

Whatever your reasons for smiling when you think of a bagel, you can be certain that eating bagels will make you a happier person. If you've never put anything but lox and cream cheese on a bagel, you're going to learn a lot of new tricks in this book. It contains everything you ever wanted to know about bagels, including how to bake your own.

Now, say "bagel." See how the word leaves your lips in a friendly smile. With this book I wish you a bagel good time!

Warmly,

June Roth

June Roth

To Lisa, a joyful bonus

Contents

History of the Bagel // 9

Bagels: A Natural Health Food // 13

Bagel Buffet Plan // 17

How to Bake a Bagel // 21

Fish on a Bagel // 25

Meat on a Bagel // 41

Poultry on a Bagel // 55

Egg on a Bagel // 63

Cheese on a Bagel // 73

Vegetables on a Bagel // 81

Hors d'Oeuvre Bagels // 89

Index // 94

History of the Bagel

History of the Bagel

It is hardly possible that you have never seen a bagel, for the boom in bagels has made them available in almost every supermarket in the country. In case this is news to you, a bagel is a round bread product with a hole in the middle. It has a shiny crust and a chewy texture, as a result of being boiled before it is baked.

The American Jewish community has been credited with the popularization of the bagel, but it has been part of culinary history for about three hundred years.

The bagel originated in Vienna, Austria, in 1683. At that time, Jan Sobieski, the king of Poland, drove off a horde of Turkish invaders. The Turks retreated so fast that they left behind thousands of sacks of green coffee. A Polish adventurer who was familiar with Italian coffeehouses acquired this coffee and established the first Viennese coffeehouse. A local bread called *kipfel,* shaped like a half-moon, was served with the coffee until the enterprising coffeehouse owner reshaped the *kipfel* to resemble the king's stirrup. The new creation was called a *beugel*, derived from the German word for stirrup, *Bügel.*

After the second partition of Poland, many Jews left Austria and Germany for Galicia, bringing their ethnic foods with them. At the time the *beugel* was circular with a hole in the middle, just as it is today. Descendants of these Jewish emigrants came to America and founded the first *beugel* bakeries in New York City. It wasn't long before the name was Americanized to *bagel*.

In Europe, the *beugel* was a treat because it was made with white flour; poor people generally ate coarse black bread. In America, the bagel was served mainly for Sunday breakfast in Jewish homes in the New York area. The traditional way of serving it was to spread the bagel halves generously with cream cheese topped with thin strips of smoked salmon, or lox. Some people added thick slices of tomato or thin slices of sweet onion before closing the sandwich.

By the 1960's, the bagel had become very popular in America; New York City had thirty bagel bakeries, and there were ten other bakeries elsewhere in the country. Lender's Bagel Bakery, in West Haven, Connecticut, introduced the first frozen bagel in 1963 and shipped it coast to coast. Consumers from all ethnic backgrounds started to eat bagels. Today, some four hundred bagel bakeries are operating throughout the country, and frozen bagels are available in most supermarkets.

From the time of the Greeks, people have thought that anything round had a perfect shape. Perhaps that explains the secret satisfaction of biting into a bagel—it is one bite of this round world and the round cycle of life that is always nutritious and delicious.

Bagels: A Natural Health Food

Bagels: A Natural Health Food

Bagels are a four-star natural food selection. The distinctive taste of a bagel depends on fresh ingredients, so they contain no artificial additives or preservatives to enhance flavor or retard spoilage. They don't need it. Bagels are eaten soon after baking or are frozen until they can be warmed and eaten later.

The ingredients in a bagel are few; it doesn't take much to make a bagel—some flour (unbleached, whole wheat, rye, or a combination), yeast, water, sugar, and salt. Your local bakery may add malt for flavor. Read the labels of other bread products you buy, then compare.

Dieters can play the interesting game of how many slices can you get out of one bagel. The average 2.3-ounce bagel has about 160 calories, so half a bagel has about 80 calories. If you can slice each bagel half into four parts, you could have a thin round of bagel for a mere 20 calories. Many health spas use these thin discs as a tasty base for low-fat cottage cheese or melted cheese.

Compared with other bread and coffee-break choices, the bagel is again a winner. Analyze the following chart and you'll see what a high-protein, low-fat, no-cholesterol, average-carbohydrate offering a bagel is.

Nutritional Information of Generally Available Packaged Products

	Serving size	Calories	Protein	Fat	Carbohydrate	Cholesterol
Plain bagel	2.3 oz	160	6 g	1 g	31 g	0 g
English muffin	2 oz	130	4 g	1 g	27 g	0 g
White bread (2 slices)	2 oz	150	5g	2 g	27 g	1.66 mg
Whole wheat bread (2 slices)	2 oz	158	4.5 g	3 g	26 g	0 g
Donut	2 oz	227	2.7 g	1 1 g	30 g	4 g
Hard roll	2 oz	190	6 g	2 g	35 g	0 g
Danish pastry	2 oz	240	4.2 g	13.4 g	26 g	2 g

Bagel Buffet Plan

Bagel Buffet Plan

Bagels are versatile. They can be featured at breakfast, brunch, lunch, supper, or late-snack buffet. They can be the center of attention with traditional offerings of smoked salmon (lox) and cream cheese, sliced tomatoes, and sliced sweet onions. Or the menu can be expanded to include an array of cheese spreads, smoked fish, seafood salads, vegetable salads, marinated vegetables, and salad molds. It can be further extended to include assorted sliced cheeses, smoked meats, and egg dishes.

For best results, warm bagels just before the meal begins. Have a sharp bread knife and board nearby for easy slicing. Provide spreaders for the cheese mixtures and forks and spoons for platters.

If hot eggs are offered in poached, scrambled, or omelet form, keep them heated in a chafing dish until serving time. Cold eggs and salads with mayonnaise should be refrigerated until the last minute.

Here are lists of foods to consider when making up your bagel buffet menu:

Cheese: Cream cheese, cream cheese with chives, pimiento cheese, cottage cheese, Swiss cheese, Muenster cheese, processed American cheese, Cheddar cheese, Gruyère cheese, blue cheese, and Roquefort cheese.

Fish: Smoked salmon (lox), smoked Nova Scotia salmon (less salty lox), smoked sable fish, smoked carp, smoked whitefish, canned or poached salmon, tuna fish, sardines, tomato sardines, mackerel, gefilte fish, herring in sour cream sauce, herring in wine sauce, matjes herring, and cooked fish used for cold fish salads.

Meat: Corned beef, pastrami, salami, bologna, roast beef, roast veal, roast lamb, cooked fresh or pickled tongue, hamburger, sliced steak, and whatever other sliced hot or cold meat you desire.

Eggs: Hard-cooked eggs that are deviled or chopped into egg salad; scrambled eggs with or without herbs or bits of meat; omelets with or without chopped onions, green peppers, or other bits of cooked vegetables; poached eggs; and eggs baked in half a bagel.

Poultry: Slices of cooked chicken, turkey, or duckling; and salads made from any of these cooked meats.

Vegetables: Sliced tomatoes, sliced cucumbers, sliced onions, potato salad, cole slaw, macaroni salad, Greek salad, and any cold vegetable salad combination that seems compatible.

Desserts: Sliced fresh melon, strawberries, blueberries, sliced oranges, grapefruit segments, coffee cake, babka cake, Danish pastries, apple strudel, cheese strudel, sliced sponge cake, and any other pick-up or sliced cake that is not iced or very rich.

How to Bake a Bagel

How to Bake a Bagel

Baking a batch of bagels requires learning a few extra steps beyond the usual techniques needed to bake bread at home. After the bagels are shaped, they are raised again, then boiled in water for a few minutes before the final step of baking. The tantalizing aroma and good taste are worth the effort needed for this interesting kitchen craft.

The most important factor in baking any bread is to be sure that the yeast is fresh and active. There are two kinds of yeast. An envelope of *active dry yeast* dissolves quickly upon stirring into liquid. Active dry yeast by the way, has an expiration date stamped on the package. *Compressed yeast* must be crumbled into liquid and then watched to be sure that some bubbling action occurs. This is called "proofing" the yeast and nowadays has to be done only with compressed yeast. Be sure to warm the liquid according to recipe directions before adding yeast, as both kinds work best when the liquid is between 105° and 115° F.

After adding the flour to the liquid solution, the yeast cells have to be worked all the way through the dough. This is known as "kneading." Dough can be kneaded with the dough-hook attachment of an electric mixer, with a hand-cranked bread maker, or by pushing and folding the dough with the heels of the palms of your hands.

The kneading job is done when the dough loses its sticky feeling and takes on a smooth and satiny texture. You may have to add a little more flour to achieve the proper elasticity, since the gluten factor varies from one batch of flour to another and cannot be measured exactly. It's best to start with a half cup less flour than the recipe calls for, then add a little more until you attain a good texture as you knead the dough.

After kneading, the dough must rest in a warm place, free of drafts, to rise properly. You might choose to set the bowl in an unheated oven with a large pan of hot water beneath it, or set it near, but not on, a range or radiator. It helps to cover the bowl with a clean linen dish towel and then let the dough rise undisturbed.

In the warm area of about 80° F., the bagels require only 15 minutes for the first rising. If permitted to rise longer, the dough may become difficult to shape and handle.

Work quickly when you divide the dough and form it into circles. Then time the second rising for about 20 minutes. A large soup pot is a good container for the boiling step—after 2 minutes, if any bagels are still on the bottom of the pot, loosen the edges with a spoon to be sure the bagel is not sticking to the bottom. At about this time, the bagels should be popping up to the surface, much like dumplings do. If you overboil the bagels, they may be soggy after baking.

Bake according to recipe directions. Place extras in a plastic bag and freeze for later use. You're going to be surprised to discover how easy it is to bake your own bagels.

Homemade Bagels

$1\frac{1}{2}$ cups warm water (about 110° F.)
    1 package active dry yeast or 1 cake compressed yeast
    2 tablespoons sugar
    1 tablespoon salt
$4\frac{1}{2}$ cups unsifted flour, (approximately)

Rinse a large bowl under hot water to warm it. Pour in the warm water. Sprinkle or crumble yeast on top of water; stir until dissolved. Stir in sugar, salt, and 4 cups of the flour to make a soft dough. Turn out onto a lightly floured board and knead about 10 minutes (adding flour to board as needed) until dough is smooth and elastic. Place in a greased bowl and turn once to grease the top of the dough. Cover bowl with a cloth and set in a warm place to rise, for 15 minutes. Punch down dough and roll on a lightly floured board into a 9 x 5-inch rectangle about 1 inch thick. Cut into 12 equal strips with a floured knife. Roll each strip into a $\frac{1}{2}$-inch-thick rope and fasten ends to form a circle. Place on a greased cookie sheet, cover, and let rise in a warm place for 20 minutes. Bring 1 gallon of water to a boil in a large pot, lower heat, and add 4 bagels. When bagels pop to the top of the water (about 2 to 3 minutes), remove to an ungreased cookie sheet. Repeat method to cook the remaining bagels. Bake in a preheated 375° F. oven 30 to 35 minutes, until browned. *Makes 1 dozen.*

Variation: Sprinkle poppy seeds, sesame seeds, dried onion flakes, minced garlic, or coarse salt over the tops of bagels while they are still wet from boiling. Allow bagels to cool before eating.

Fish on a Bagel

Lox And Cream Cheese Bagel

What would a bagel book be without a lox and cream cheese recipe? It's the traditional way to serve a bagel, and loved for good reason.

        4 bagels, cut in half
        1 package (3-ounce) cream cheese
    ¼ pound sliced smoked salmon
        4 thin slices sweet onion (optional)
        4 slices tomato (optional)

Spread bagel bottoms with cream cheese. Cover with smoked salmon. Add onion and tomato if desired. Spread bagel tops with remaining cream cheese and cover sandwiches. *Makes 4 servings.*

Lox Spread Bagel

This is a good way to stretch a small amount of smoked salmon. Chives give it extra flavor.

        1 package (3-ounce) cream cheese
        1 tablespoon dairy sour cream
        2 slices smoked salmon, chopped fine
        1 tablespoon chopped chives (optional)
        4 bagels, cut in half
        4 slices tomato

Mash together cream cheese and sour cream until cheese is fluffy. Add chopped smoked salmon and chives. Spread thickly on bagel bottoms. Cover with tomato slices and then with bagel tops. *Makes 4 servings.*

Swiss Nova Bagel

Nova Scotia smoked salmon has a more delicate flavor and is less salty than regular lox. This traditional combination is a favorite of many.

4 poppy seed bagels, cut in half
1 package (3-ounce) cream cheese
4 slices Nova Scotia smoked salmon
4 slices Swiss cheese
4 slices sweet onion

Spread all bagel halves with cream cheese. Arrange Nova salmon on bagel bottoms. Add Swiss cheese and then onion. Cover with bagel tops. *Makes 4 servings.*

Nova Bagel Soufflé

You'll find this a wonderful selection for a brunch or luncheon menu. The puffy topping covers a dainty filling to everyone's pleasure.

2 bagels, cut in half
$\frac{1}{4}$ pound Nova Scotia smoked salmon
$\frac{1}{4}$ pound cooked asparagus, drained and cut in half
$\frac{2}{3}$ cup mayonnaise
$\frac{1}{4}$ cup grated Swiss cheese
1 teaspoon grated onion
$\frac{1}{4}$ teaspoon salt
2 egg whites

Arrange the bagel halves in a baking dish. Top with slices of Nova salmon. Arrange asparagus pieces in a row over salmon. Combine mayonnaise, Swiss cheese, grated onion, and salt. Beat egg whites until stiff peaks form; fold into mayonnaise mixture. Spread lightly over asparagus. Set broiler about 6 inches from heat. Broil prepared bagels for 5 minutes, or until tops are lightly browned. *Makes 4 servings.*

Lox Fin Bagel

In the New York region this fin is called the "lox head."
This doesn't make too much sense, but the
recipe using it does.

 3 tablespoons olive oil
 2 onions, sliced thin
 1 lox fin
 4 pumpernickel bagels, cut in half

Heat oil in skillet. Sauté onions until limp. Add lox fin and cover skillet. Cook over low heat for 20 minutes. Remove lox fin and discard skin and bones. Shred remaining cooked lox and mix with sautéed onions. Pile mixture on bagel bottoms and cover sandwiches. *Makes 4 servings.*

Red Caviar Bagel

Red caviar is the roe of salmon and is available in small jars in the gourmet section of the supermarket. It's especially delicious served this way.

 1 package (3-ounce) cream cheese
 1 small jar red caviar, drained
 1 tablespoon chopped chives
 ½ teaspoon dried dill weed
 ½ teaspoon lemon juice
 4 pumpernickel bagels, cut in half

Mash cream cheese until fluffy. Add caviar, chives, dill weed, and lemon juice; mix thoroughly but do not break the caviar eggs. Pile onto bagel bottoms and cover with bagel tops. *Makes 4 servings.*

Sturgeon Bagel

Smoked sturgeon, a great delicacy, is also expensive. This bagel idea makes use of a small amount in a tasteful way.

4 rye bagels, cut in half
1½ ounces (½ small package) cream cheese
4 slices smoked sturgeon
4 slices Muenster cheese
4 slices tomato

Spread bagel bottoms with cream cheese. Cover with sturgeon, then a layer of Muenster cheese, and finally tomato slices. Cover sandwiches with bagel tops. *Makes 4 servings.*

Whitefish Cheese Bagel

Buy a small smoked whitefish at your local delicatessen and carefully remove the fish meat from the bones. The bones are sharp, so a feel here and there will prevent a problem. The marvelous taste is worth the extra effort.

1 package (8-ounce) chive cream cheese
1 tablespoon dairy sour cream
4 rye bagels, cut in half
¼ pound boneless smoked whitefish
4 slices tomato

Mash together cream cheese and sour cream until fluffy. Spread on all bagel halves. Arrange whitefish pieces on bagel bottoms. Top with tomato slices. Cover with bagel tops. *Makes 4 servings.*

Smoked Sablefish Bagel

Sablefish is found along the Pacific coast and is sometimes called black codfish. It's a delicacy when smoked and requires little enhancement.

1 package (8-ounce) chive cream cheese
1 teaspoon lemon juice
4 rye bagels, cut in half
$\frac{1}{4}$ pound smoked sablefish
4 slices tomato

Mash together cream cheese and lemon juice. Spread generously on all bagel halves. Arrange small pieces of sablefish over cheese on bottom halves. Add tomato slices. Cover with top halves. *Makes 4 servings.*

Fish Salad Bagel

When there's just a cup of cooked fish left over, here's a perky salad to use it up. Stretches to serve four people too.

1 cup flaked cooked fish
2 hard-cooked eggs, chopped
$\frac{1}{2}$ dill pickle, finely chopped
$\frac{1}{4}$ cup finely diced celery
$\frac{1}{2}$ small onion, finely diced
$\frac{1}{4}$ cup mayonnaise
4 bagels, cut in half
4 slices tomato

Combine fish, eggs, pickle, celery, onion, and mayonnaise; mix well. Spread on bagel bottoms. Cover with tomato slices. Spread additional mayonnaise on bagel tops and cover sandwiches. *Makes 4 servings.*

Tempura Bagel

Feel free to cut up vegetables other than those mentioned here, and dip them in batter to deep-fry. The crunchy crust is mouthwateringly good.

1 egg	8 small pieces fish fillets
½ cup water	8 sprigs fresh parsley
1 cup cake flour	16 thin slices zucchini
½ teaspoon salt	8 bagels, cut in half
Oil for deep-frying	

Beat egg slightly; add water and mix well. Gradually stir in cake flour; mix only until almost all lumps are dissolved. Add salt. Heat oil to 320° F., or until a small amount of batter dropped from a spoon into oil browns quickly. Dip pieces of fish, parsley, and zucchini into batter and deep-fry a few at a time until all are lightly browned and puffed. Remove from pan and place on paper toweling to drain until all are done. Place one piece of fish, two pieces of zucchini, and a parsley sprig on a bagel bottom. Sprinkle with soy sauce, if desired. Cover with bagel top and serve. *Makes 8 servings.*

Fishburger Bagel

You don't have to go to a fast-food place to get a good fried fish sandwich. Make your own and enjoy it twice as much.

1 egg	¼ cup cooking oil
1 tablespoon lemon juice	6 bagels, cut in half
½ teaspoon salt	Shredded lettuce
3 small fish fillets, cut in half	¼ cup mayonnaise
½ cup Italian seasoned bread crumbs	2 tablespoons chopped cucumber
	¼ teaspoon dried dill weed

Beat together egg, lemon juice, and salt. Dip pieces of fish into egg and then coat with bread crumbs. Heat oil in a skillet. Fry coated fish until golden on both sides, 5 to 10 minutes. Place a piece of fish on each bagel bottom. Top with shredded lettuce. Combine mayonnaise, chopped cucumber, and dill weed; spread on bagel tops and cover sandwiches. *Makes 6 servings.*

Fish Stick Bagel

Here's a quick way to prepare a meal from the freezer. It's filling and much less expensive than the ones from the fast-food places.

8 frozen fish sticks	Shredded lettuce
4 bagels, cut in half	4 slices tomato
Tartar sauce	Sliced sweet pickle

Heat fish sticks according to package directions. Spread all bagel halves with tartar sauce. Place two hot fish sticks on each bagel bottom. Top with shredded lettuce, tomato, and sliced pickle. Cover with bagel tops and serve at once. *Makes 4 servings.*

Gefilte Fish Bagel

You can purchase gefilte fish in jars or cans at the supermarket. It's a poached fish ball similar to the French quenelle.

- $\frac{1}{4}$ cup mayonnaise
- $\frac{1}{2}$ teaspoon white horseradish
- $\frac{1}{4}$ teaspoon dried dillweed
- 4 bagels, cut in half
  Shredded lettuce
- 2 pieces gefilte fish
- 4 slices tomato

Combine mayonnaise, horseradish, and dillweed. Spread on all bagel halves. Arrange a layer of shredded lettuce on 4 bagel bottoms. Cut gefilte fish in half lengthwise; arrange one piece on each bed of lettuce. Top with tomato and cover with remaining bagel halves. *Makes 4 servings.*

Grilled Tuna Bagel

There's nothing like finding a tuna surprise under melted cheese. Serve this open-face sandwich with a knife and fork.

- 1 can (7-ounce) tuna fish, drained
- 2 tablespoons mayonnaise
- $\frac{1}{4}$ teaspoon dried oregano
- $\frac{1}{4}$ teaspoon garlic powder
- 3 bagels, cut in half
- 6 slices tomato
- 6 slices Muenster cheese

Combine tuna fish, mayonnaise, oregano, and garlic powder; mash well. Spread on all bagel halves. Top with a tomato slice and then with cheese. Slip under the broiler until cheese melts. *Makes 6 servings.*

Tuna Chutney Bagel

Chutney is an Indian mixture made with fruit and spices. Add a little powdered curry if you want to feel like a rajah.

1 can (7-ounce) tuna fish, drained
2 tablespoons mayonnaise
¼ cup chutney
1 teaspoon chopped parsley
4 poppy seed bagels, cut in half
1 cup finely shredded red cabbage
Mayonnaise

Mash together tuna fish, mayonnaise, chutney and chopped parsley. Spread on bagel bottoms. Top with shredded red cabbage. Spread additional mayonnaise on bagel tops and cover sandwiches. *Makes 4 servings.*

Tuna Pepper Bagel

This sandwich makes a good lunch for brown-baggers or stay-at-homes. Crunchy and nutritious too.

1 can (7-ounce) tuna, drained
2 tablespoons mayonnaise
½ stalk celery, diced fine
½ green pepper, seeded and diced fine
4 bagels, cut in half

Mash together tuna, mayonnaise, celery, and green pepper. Spread on bagel bottoms. Spread additional mayonnaise on bagel tops if desired. Cover with tops. *Makes 4 servings.*

Tuna Avocado Bagel

Avocado lends an air of sophistication to this recipe. Be sure to pick a ripe avocado, then root the pit and start a new houseplant for free.

1 can (7-ounce) tuna fish
¼ cup chopped celery
2 tablespoons chopped, pitted black olives
¼ cup mayonnaise
¼ teaspoon curry powder
2 sesame seed bagels, cut in half
8 thin slices ripe avocado
4 slices Cheddar cheese

Combine tuna, celery, and olives. Stir mayonnaise and curry powder together; add to tuna mixture. Spread on all bagel halves. Top with avocado slices and then Cheddar cheese. Broil until cheese melts. *Makes 4 servings.*

Tuna Cheese Bagel

Here's a lovely tuna and cheese combination with a zesty horseradish sauce. Add sliced tomato, shredded lettuce, or both if you wish.

1 can (7-ounce) tuna, drained
¼ cup cottage cheese
1 tablespoon mayonnaise
1 tablespoon dairy sour cream

1 tablespoon finely chopped onion
1 teaspoon horseradish
¼ teaspoon Worcestershire sauce
4 bagels, cut in half

Combine tuna, cottage cheese, mayonnaise, sour cream, chopped onion, horseradish, and Worcestershire sauce until well mixed. Spread bagel bottoms with mixture. Cover with tops. *Makes 4 servings.*

Tuna Pineapple Bagel

If you're tired of plain tuna fish, pep it up with crushed pineapple. It's easy and it's so good!

    1 can (7-ounce) tuna, drained
    2 tablespoons canned crushed pineapple
    2 tablespoons mayonnaise
    4 bagels, cut in half
    4 pieces lettuce
      Mayonnaise

Mash together tuna, crushed pineapple, and mayonnaise. Spread mixture on bagel bottoms, then add lettuce pieces. Spread additional mayonnaise on bagel tops and cover sandwiches. *Makes 4 servings.*

Salmon Cheese Bagel

This recipe stretches expensive canned salmon to feed four in a most appetizing way. The thinly sliced cucumbers give an extra pleasing taste.

      1 can (7-ounce) salmon, drained
   $1\frac{1}{2}$ ounces ($\frac{1}{2}$ small package) cream cheese
     $\frac{1}{2}$ teaspoon dill weed
      2 tablespoons mayonnaise
      1 small cucumber, peeled and thinly sliced
      4 rye bagels, cut in half
        Mayonnaise

Mash together salmon and cream cheese. Add dill weed and mayonnaise. Spread on bagel bottoms. Top with cucumber slices. Spread additional mayonnaise on bagel tops and cover sandwiches. *Makes 4 servings.*

Tomato Sardine Bagel

Don't skip the lemon juice—it brings out the delicate flavor of the sardines. Great with pumpernickel bagels.

1 can (8-ounce) tomato sardines
1 tablespoon lemon juice
1 hard-cooked egg, chopped
1 teaspoon grated onion
2 tablespoons mayonnaise

4 pumpernickel bagels,
  cut in half
  Shredded lettuce
  Mayonnaise

Remove bones from sardines, drain well, and mash with lemon juice. Add chopped egg, onion, and mayonnaise. Spread on bagel bottoms, then add shredded lettuce. Spread bagel tops with additional mayonnaise and cover sandwiches. *Makes 4 servings.*

Tomato Herring Bagel

It's a wise homemaker who keeps a few cans of tomato herring tucked away on a pantry shelf. So easy to mash into a no-nonsense spread.

1 can (14-ounce) herring in tomato sauce	1 tablespoon grated onion
1 tablespoon mayonnaise	6 bagels, cut in half
1 teaspoon lemon juice	6 slices tomato
1/4 teaspoon dried dill weed	6 pieces lettuce
	Mayonnaise

Drain juice from herring and discard juice. Mash herring with mayonnaise, lemon juice, dill weed, and grated onion. Spread mixture on bagel bottoms, then add a slice of tomato and a piece of lettuce to each spread. Spread additional mayonnaise on bagel tops if desired. Cover sandwiches with bagel tops. *Makes 6 servings.*

Mackerel Cheese Bagel

You might not think of canned mackerel when you're preparing your marketing list, but it's a good staple to consider. Tastes somewhat like a sardine, but better.

1 can (4$\frac{3}{8}$-ounce) skinless and boneless mackerel fillets
4 garlic bagels, cut in half
4 slices processed American cheese
4 thin slices red onion
Softened butter

Drain juice from mackerel and discard juice. Arrange mackerel fillets on bagel bottoms. Cover with a slice of cheese and a slice of red onion. Spread butter on bagel tops and cover sandwiches. *Makes 4 servings.*

Sardine Bagel

Pay a little more and buy skinless and boneless sardines. It's the difference between mundane and marvelous.

1 can (3¾-ounce) skinless and
   boneless sardines, drained
1 tablespoon tartar sauce
4 onion bagels, cut in half
4 whole pimientos
   Softened butter

Mash sardines with tartar sauce. Spread on bagel bottoms. Cover with whole pimientos. Spread bagel tops with butter and cover sandwiches.
Makes 4 servings.

Anchovy Caper Bagel

You may have to search your supermarket's shelves for these caper-stuffed rolled anchovies, but it will be worth the effort. A gourmet's delight!

1 package (8-ounce) cream cheese
1 tablespoon dairy sour cream
1 tablespoon sweet relish
4 rye bagels, cut in half
1 can (2-ounce) rolled anchovy fillets
   stuffed with capers

Mash together cream cheese, sour cream, and sweet relish. Spread on all bagel halves. Arrange anchovy fillets around bottom halves. Cover with bagel tops.
Makes 4 servings.

Chopped Herring Bagel

If you're in a hurry, drain a large-size jar of herring in wine sauce and substitute it in this recipe. Either way, it's a tangy treat.

1 herring, preferably fresh or matjes	2 tablespoons vinegar
	$\frac{1}{4}$ teaspoon pepper
2 hard-cooked eggs	1 teaspoon sugar
1 onion, cut up	4 bagels, cut in half
1 apple, peeled and cored	4 lettuce leaves

Soak the herring overnight; remove skin and bones, and clean. Chop herring, eggs, onion, and apple very fine. Add vinegar, pepper, and sugar. Spread mixture thickly on bagel bottoms, cover with lettuce, then with bagel tops. Chill any remaining chopped herring until needed. *Makes 4 servings.*

Beet 'n' Herring Bagel

This combination was inspired by a Swedish dish but would be at home in Russia, too. The bagel adapts to so many ethnic foods.

4 pumpernickel bagels, cut in half
  Softened butter
1 herring in cream sauce with onions
$\frac{1}{2}$ teaspoon dried dill weed
$\frac{1}{2}$ cup sliced pickled beets

Spread all bagel halves with a thin layer of butter. Cut herring into bite-size pieces. With a slotted spoon, allowing most of the cream sauce to drain off, arrange herring bits and onions on bagel bottoms. Sprinkle with dill weed. Add a layer of pickled beets. Cover sandwiches with buttered bagel tops. *Makes 4 servings.*

Meat on a Bagel

Corned Beef 'n' Cabbage Salad Bagel

This is an excellent cole slaw recipe with just the right balance of sweet and sour. Adding diced corned beef makes it a meal in one.

1 cup shredded cabbage	$\frac{1}{4}$ cup dairy sour cream
1 tablespoon finely chopped celery	1 teaspoon lemon juice
1 tablespoon finely chopped green pepper	1 teaspoon sugar
1 teaspoon finely chopped onion	4 slices cooked corned beef, diced
$\frac{1}{4}$ cup mayonnaise	4 pumpernickel bagels, cut in half
	Mustard

Combine cabbage, celery, green pepper, and chopped onion. Then combine mayonnaise, sour cream, lemon juice, and sugar; mix until smooth. Pour liquid over cabbage mixture and toss well. Refrigerate cabbage mixture for several hours. Add diced corned beef to mixture just before serving. Spread bagel tops with mustard and cover sandwiches. *Makes 4 servings.*

Hot Pastrami Bagel

This is a superb combination. It will make you want to eat more than you should.

4 rye bagels, cut in half	4 slices cooked turkey
Mustard	Shredded lettuce
$\frac{1}{2}$ pound sliced hot pastrami	Russian dressing

Spread bagel bottoms with a thin layer of mustard. Cover with a thick layer of sliced hot pastrami, then with turkey. Top with shredded lettuce. Spread Russian dressing on bagel tops and cover sandwiches. *Makes 4 servings.*

Hero Bagel

You might want to add a layer of sliced cheese to this combination. Swiss, Muenster or provolone will do nicely.

$\frac{1}{8}$ pound sliced salami
$\frac{1}{8}$ pound sliced roast beef
4 sliced green pepper rings
4 slices sweet onion
4 onion bagels, cut in half
$\frac{1}{4}$ cup Russian dressing

Arrange layers of salami, roast beef, green pepper, and onion on each bagel bottom. Spread Russian dressing on each bagel top and place on filling. *Makes 4 servings.*

Reuben Bagel

Here's a famous sandwich grilled in a bagel. Make your Reuben open-face if you wish; provide knives and forks for easier eating.

4 rye bagels, cut in half
$\frac{1}{2}$ pound lean corned beef, sliced thin
1 cup sauerkraut, drained
4 slices Swiss cheese

On bagel bottoms arrange sliced corned beef, tucking ends under. Spread drained sauerkraut over beef. Top with Swiss cheese, tucking ends under. Broil until cheese melts. Cover with bagel tops and broil a moment to heat tops. Serve at once. *Makes 4 servings.*

Melted Swiss Tongue Bagel

Conventional sliced tongue takes on a party air when it's topped with cheese and grilled. Add some chopped green pepper to the onion if you wish.

4 poppy seed bagels, cut in half	½ cup coarsely chopped Swiss cheese
Mustard	2 tablespoons finely chopped onion
8 slices cooked tongue	

Spread bagel bottoms with a thin layer of mustard. Cover with tongue. Combine Swiss cheese and chopped onion; spread over tongue. Broil until cheese melts. Cover with bagel tops and broil a moment to heat through. Serve at once. *Makes 4 servings.*

Bagel Grinder

This Italian-style sandwich has layers of surprises, and you can tuck in a few of your own. Creativity at its best.

4 bagels, cut in half
   Mayonnaise
8 slices salami
4 slices provolone cheese
4 slices onion
4 slices tomato
   Shredded lettuce
   Olive oil

Spread bagel bottoms with mayonnaise. Cover each bottom half with two slices of salami and a slice of cheese, onion, and tomato. Top with shredded lettuce. Drizzle olive oil over lettuce. Cover with bagel tops. *Makes 4 servings.*

Bologna Stack Bagels

Cut into wedges, this recipe can be used for hors d'oeuvres; as is, it's a good lunch. Either way, it's a neat way to serve bologna.

> 1 package (3-ounce) cream cheese
> 2 tablespoons dairy sour cream
> $\frac{1}{2}$ cup chopped stuffed olives
> $\frac{1}{4}$ teaspoon garlic powder
> 4 pumpernickel bagels, cut in half
> 20 slices bologna

Mash together cream cheese and sour cream until mixture is soft and creamy. Add olives and garlic powder. Spread a thin layer on each bagel bottom, then cover with a bologna slice. Spread a thin layer of cheese mixture over bologna slice and top with another bologna slice. Continue layering, ending with a thin layer of cheese mixture. Cover with bagel tops. *Makes 4 servings.*

Bologna Bagel

You can buy whole pimientos in a jar, usually in the pickle aisle of your supermarket. Refrigerate leftovers for imaginative use another day.

> 2 rye bagels, cut in half
> 6 slices bologna
> 2 whole pimientos
> Shredded lettuce
> Mustard

Cover bagel bottoms with bologna, place a pimiento on each, and top with shredded lettuce. Spread mustard on bagel tops and cover sandwiches. *Makes 2 servings.*

Hobo Bagel

There's a treat in every mouthful, and kids love it. Serve a salad or cole slaw on the side.

> 6 frankfurters
> 6 rye bagels, cut in half
> 1 can (16-ounce) baked beans, heated
> ⅓ cup shredded Cheddar cheese
> Mustard

Boil frankfurters, then cut them in half crosswise and again horizontally. Arrange on bagel bottoms. Top with several spoonfuls of hot baked beans and then with shredded cheese. Spread mustard on bagel tops and cover sandwiches. *Makes 6 servings.*

Meatball Bagel

Here's a great idea for a supper night when the family's on the run. Keep the meatballs warm and let everyone spoon out a portion between appointments.

1 can (16-ounce) tomatoes in tomato sauce
1 can (6-ounce) tomato paste
½ teaspoon oregano
1 clove garlic, minced fine
1 pound ground beef
1 egg
½ cup seasoned Italian bread crumbs
1 small onion, grated
2 tablespoons chopped parsley
1 tablespoon grated Parmesan cheese
6 bagels, cut in half

Empty tomatoes and tomato paste into a deep saucepan. Add oregano and garlic. Cook over low heat. Combine ground beef, egg, bread crumbs, onion, parsley, and Parmesan cheese; mix well. Form into bite-size meatballs. Add meatballs to tomato sauce, cover and simmer for 45 minutes. Spoon meatballs and sauce over bagel bottoms. Cover with bagel tops. *Makes 6 servings.*

Wimpy Bagel

If you spread the meat mixture thin on the bagel, it cooks to perfection in just a few minutes. And all the juices are caught in the bagel. Yum!

1 pound ground beef   2 tablespoons catsup
½ onion, grated   4 onion bagels, cut in half

Combine ground beef, grated onion, and catsup; mix well. Spread all bagel halves with beef mixture. Slip under broiler for several minutes, until browned. *Makes 4 servings of 2 halves each.*

Giant Sloppy Joe Bagel

You can make your own super-size bagel with the recipe for Homemade Bagels (see Index) or order one at your local bagel bakery. This makes a great centerpiece for a casual buffet. Garnish with dill pickles and have a bowl of potato salad nearby.

1 12-inch bagel, cut in half	$\frac{1}{2}$ pound sliced, cooked turkey
1 pound sliced, cooked corned beef	$\frac{1}{2}$ pound cole slaw, well-drained
$\frac{1}{2}$ pound sliced bologna	Russian dressing
$\frac{1}{2}$ pound sliced, cooked tongue	Parsley for garnish

Place bagel bottom on a large platter. Cover with a layer of corned beef, then bologna, then tongue, and finally turkey. Spread a thin layer of well-drained cole slaw over turkey. Spread bagel top with Russian dressing and cover sandwich. Cut into 12 segments. Garnish with parsley. *Makes 12 servings.*

Frankfurter Bagel

Sure you've heard of sauerkraut on a frankfurter, but have you ever tried this applesauce trick? The bagel makes it a heartier meal.

4 boiled or grilled frankfurters
4 sesame seed bagels, cut in half
$\frac{1}{4}$ cup applesauce
1 cup sauerkraut, drained
Mustard

Cut hot frankfurters in half crosswise and then horizontally; arrange in a layer on bagel bottoms. Spread a layer of applesauce and then a layer of sauerkraut over frankfurters. Spread mustard on bagel tops and cover sandwiches. *Makes 4 servings.*

Apricot Frank Bagel

Once you've tasted frankfurters this way, you'll never eat them plain again. It's a sweet way with a hotdog!

24 cocktail frankfurters
$\frac{1}{4}$ cup apricot jam
1 teaspoon prepared mustard
4 poppy seed bagels, cut in half

Boil tiny frankfurters until tender. Drain well. Combine apricot jam and mustard; toss with frankfurters in saucepan. Heat until jam melts and mixture is hot. Spoon onto bagel bottoms and place bagel tops over all. *Makes 4 servings.*

Bagelburger

Why not use a bagel instead of a hamburger bun? It's a firmer base for the burger.

$\frac{1}{2}$ pound lean ground beef
$\frac{1}{4}$ teaspoon garlic salt
$\frac{1}{4}$ teaspoon salt
$\frac{1}{8}$ teaspoon pepper
2 tablespoons cold water

1 small onion, sliced
1 tablespoon olive oil
    Dash Worcestershire sauce
2 onion bagels, cut in half

Combine ground beef, garlic salt, salt, pepper, and cold water. Mix lightly and form into two hamburger patties. Broil, turning once, until done to your taste. Meanwhile, heat oil in small skillet; sauté onion until translucent, stirring occasionally. Add Worcestershire sauce. Place cooked hamburgers on bagel bottoms, add onions, and cover with tops. *Makes 2 servings.*

French Onion Steak Bagel

Here's a nice idea for leftover sliced steak when you're not sure if there's enough to go around. The onion rings add a different touch!

4 poppy seed bagels,
   cut in half
   Mayonnaise
8 thin slices cold cooked steak
$\frac{1}{2}$ cup canned French-fried onion rings
   Shredded lettuce
   Catsup

Spread bagel bottoms with a thin layer of mayonnaise. Cover with steak slices and then with French-fried onion rings. Add shredded lettuce. Spread catsup on bagel tops and cover sandwiches. *Makes 4 sandwiches.*

Hash on a Bagel

How can you stretch leftover boiled potatoes and cooked meat to serve eight hungry people? Make hash and serve it on a bagel. For extra protein, top each bagel with a poached egg.

3 tablespoons butter
   or margarine
2 medium onions, diced fine
$1\frac{1}{2}$ pounds cold boiled
   potatoes, diced

1 pound cooked meat, diced
$\frac{1}{4}$ teaspoon salt
$\frac{1}{8}$ teaspoon pepper
$\frac{1}{8}$ teaspoon dried mustard
4 bagels, cut in half

Melt butter in a large skillet. Sauté onions until limp. Add diced potatoes, meat, salt, pepper, and mustard. Cook until browned on one side, turn carefully, and brown other side. Place half a bagel on each plate and spoon hot hash over it. *Makes 8 servings.*

Chili Con Carne Bagel

If you're a chili freak, add more chili powder to suit your taste buds. However you do it, it's bound to be a zesty offering.

2 tablespoons olive oil
2 onions, thinly sliced
1 pound ground beef
2 teaspoons chili powder
1 teaspoon salt
½ teaspoon paprika
¼ teaspoon Tabasco sauce
1 can (16-ounce) tomatoes
1 can (6-ounce) tomato paste
1 can (20-ounce) kidney beans
4 bagels, cut in half

Heat oil in a large skillet. Sauté onions until tender. Add ground beef, breaking it apart with a fork while it browns. Sprinkle with chili powder, salt, paprika, and Tabasco sauce. Add tomatoes and tomato paste. Cover and simmer 15 minutes. Add kidney beans and simmer 15 minutes longer. Arrange bagel halves on 4 plates. Spoon chili con carne over bagels and serve. *Makes 4 servings.*

Taco Bagel

Yes, you can stuff a bagel as you would a tortilla. It's hearty and tastes twice as good.

½ pound ground beef
½ head shredded lettuce
1 tomato, diced
1½ cups grated Cheddar cheese
½ cup mayonnaise
1 teaspoon chili powder
8 bagels, cut in half

Brown ground beef in skillet, breaking the beef apart with a fork and stirring constantly. Cool. Combine with shredded lettuce, tomato, and grated cheese. Combine mayonnaise and chili powder; toss with meat mixture. Pile on bagel bottoms and cover with bagel tops. *Makes 8 servings.*

Roast Beef Bagel

Why use cottony white bread for your leftover roast beef sandwiches when you can serve nutritious bagels that taste so much better? Get smart!

4 poppy seed bagels, cut in half
¼ cup Russian dressing
4 slices cooked roast beef
4 slices Swiss cheese
4 lettuce leaves

Spread bagel bottoms with some of the Russian dressing. Cover with roast beef, then Swiss cheese, and finally lettuce leaves. Spread remaining Russian dressing on bagel tops and cover sandwiches. *Makes 4 servings.*

Veal and Red Cabbage Bagel

You've never thought of putting prunes on a sandwich? Try this cabbage and veal combination from the old country.

4 pumpernickel bagels, cut in half
Butter or margarine
4 thin slices cooked veal roast
$\frac{1}{2}$ cup cooked red cabbage, well-drained
8 cooked prunes, pitted and well-drained

Spread bagel bottoms with butter or margarine. Arrange veal slices on bottoms. Top with a layer of red cabbage. Cut prunes in half and arrange over cabbage. Spread additional butter or margarine on bagel tops and cover sandwiches. *Makes 4 servings.*

Veal and Peppers Bagel

Here's a wonderful way to stretch a pound of veal to serve six people. Don't forget the rosemary—it has a pungent flavor.

3 tablespoons olive oil
1 onion
1 clove garlic, finely minced
3 green peppers, seeded and
cut into 1-inch squares
1 pound veal, cubed
1 can (16-ounce) tomatoes
in sauce
1 can (6-ounce) tomato paste
$\frac{1}{2}$ teaspoon dried rosemary
$\frac{1}{2}$ teaspoon salt
$\frac{1}{4}$ teaspoon pepper
6 bagels, cut in half

Heat olive oil in a saucepan. Add onion and garlic and cook for several minutes. Add green peppers; cook and stir until peppers are limp. Add veal, stirring until all sides are browned. Add tomatoes, tomato paste, rosemary, salt, and pepper. Cover and simmer for 35 minutes, or until tender. Spoon onto bagel bottoms, then cover with bagel tops. *Makes 6 servings.*

Lamb Cucumber Bagel

When you've roasted a leg of lamb and wonder how to serve leftovers, think of this enjoyable combination. It's simple but has an elegant flavor.

$\frac{1}{4}$ cup mayonnaise

$\frac{1}{2}$ teaspoon dried dill weed

4 onion bagels, cut in half

8 very thin slices cold
   roast lamb

$\frac{1}{2}$ cucumber, sliced paper thin

Combine mayonnaise and dill weed; spread on bagel halves. Arrange 2 slices of roast lamb on each bagel bottom. Top with thin slices of cucumber. Cover with bagel tops. *Makes 4 servings.*

Poultry on a Bagel

Turkey in Horseradish Sauce Bagel

If you haven't any turkey left over from a roast, consider buying some slices of turkey breast at the deli. The whipped-cream horseradish sauce will make it worth the effort.

½ cup heavy cream, whipped
2 tablespoons horseradish
4 rye bagels, cut in half
8 thin slices cooked turkey
1 cucumber, peeled and sliced thin
4 lettuce leaves

Combine whipped cream and horseradish. Spread mixture on bagel bottoms. Top with turkey slices, then a layer of cucumbers, and finally with lettuce. Spread remaining horseradish sauce on bagel tops and cover sandwiches.

Chopped Liver Turkey Bagel

It's the combination sandwiches that taste the most interesting. This one is emphatically enchanting.

4 bagels, cut in half
¼ pound cooked chopped liver
4 slices cooked turkey
½ cup cole slaw, drained
    Russian dressing

Spread bagel bottoms with chopped liver. Cover with turkey and then with cole slaw. Spread bagel tops with Russian dressing and cover sandwiches. *Makes 4 servings.*

Note: Chopped liver may be purchased at a delicatessen or homemade.

(See Index for Chopped Liver Bagel recipe.)

Turkey Cranberry Bagel

Of course you know that turkey and cranberry sauce go well together, but did you ever try them on a bagel? You'll like it well enough to do so again and again.

4 bagels, cut in half	4 slices cooked turkey
$\frac{1}{4}$ cup mayonnaise	Shredded lettuce
$\frac{1}{4}$ teaspoon dried dill weed	$\frac{1}{2}$ cup whole cranberry sauce

Spread bagel bottoms with a mixture of mayonnaise and dill weed. Cover with sliced turkey. Top with shredded lettuce and then a layer of cranberry sauce. Cover sandwiches with bagel tops. *Makes 4 servings.*

Turkey Dagwood Bagel

If you have all these goodies in your refrigerator for late-night snackers, you'll understand why there's nothing left by morning. A bag of bagels in the freezer is sensible pantry insurance.

4 rye bagels, cut in half
4 slices cooked turkey
4 slices cooked tongue
2 hard-cooked eggs, sliced
4 slices tomato
4 slices sweet onion
   Russian dressing

On bagel bottoms arrange layers of turkey and tongue. Add layers of sliced eggs, tomato, and onion. Spread Russian dressing on bagel tops and cover sandwiches. *Makes 4 servings.*

Chicken Cheese Bagel

If the cream cheese is too stiff, soften it with a bit of dairy sour cream or milk. Brown-baggers will love you for this one.

        1 cup finely chopped cooked chicken
        1 package (3-ounce) chive
            cream cheese, softened
        ½ teaspoon salt
        4 poppy seed bagels,
            cut in half
        ½ cup sliced black olives
        4 lettuce leaves

Combine chopped chicken, chive cream cheese, and salt. Pile mixture on bagel bottoms. Add sliced olives and lettuce. Cover with bagel tops. *Makes 4 servings.*

Chicken Walnut Salad Bagel

Here's how to turn leftover chicken into a salad creation. Serve open-face if you prefer.

        2 cups cooked chicken, diced
        ¼ cup chopped celery
        ¼ cup pineapple tidbits, drained
        2 tablespoons broken walnuts
        ¼ cup mayonnaise
        ¼ teaspoon dried dill weed
        6 rye bagels, cut in half
            Mayonnaise

Combine chicken, celery, pineapple, walnuts, mayonnaise, and dill weed. Spread on bagel bottoms. Spread tops with additional mayonnaise, if desired, and cover sandwiches. *Makes 6 servings.*

Sliced Chicken Bagel

When just a plain chicken sandwich is what you have in mind, put it on a bagel. It makes the best plain chicken sandwich.

4 slices cooked chicken
4 bagels, cut in half
4 slices tomato
4 pieces lettuce
$\frac{1}{4}$ cup Russian dressing

Arrange chicken on bagel bottoms. Cover with tomato and lettuce. Spread bagel tops with Russian dressing and close sandwiches. *Makes 4 servings.*

Chicken à la King Bagel

Chicken à la king can be served in a pastry shell or on toasted bread. What a nice idea to serve it on a bagel instead.

4 tablespoons butter
$\frac{1}{2}$ pound fresh mushrooms, sliced
$\frac{1}{2}$ green pepper, chopped
1 pimiento, cut fine
3 tablespoons flour
1 cup chicken broth
$\frac{1}{2}$ cup milk
$\frac{1}{2}$ teaspoon salt
$\frac{1}{8}$ teaspoon pepper
2 egg yolks
$\frac{1}{2}$ cup heavy cream
1 teaspoon sherry
2 cups cooked chicken, diced and boned
2 bagels, cut in half

Melt butter in a heavy saucepan. Add mushrooms, pepper, and pimiento. Cook over low heat until mushrooms are limp. Stir in flour until smooth. Slowly blend in chicken broth and milk. Cook and stir until thickened. Add salt and pepper. Beat egg yolks slightly with heavy cream; add to sauce. Add sherry. Add chicken and heat through. Place a bagel half on each plate and spoon hot chicken and sauce over it. *Makes 4 servings.*

Bagel Divan

Here's a quick and easy way to make a fancy dish, using leftover sliced chicken and America's favorite condensed soup sauce. The sherry and Parmesan cheese disguise the source.

4 bagels, cut in half
2 packages (10-ounce) frozen broccoli spears, cooked
8 large slices cooked chicken
1 can (10½-ounce) condensed cream of mushroom soup
2 tablespoons milk
1 tablespoon dry sherry
2 tablespoons grated Parmesan cheese

Place bagel halves in a baking dish. Drain cooked broccoli and cut spears in half; arrange in a row on bagel halves. Cover each bagel half with 2 slices of chicken. In a small saucepan combine condensed soup, milk, sherry, and cheese; heat and stir until smooth. Spoon mixture over chicken. Bake in a 350° F. oven for 15 minutes, or until slightly browned on top. *Makes 8 servings.*

Club Bagel

Certainly cooked bacon can be used instead of corned beef. Or use both. It's your sandwich!

2 bagels, cut in half
2 slices cooked chicken
2 slices cooked corned beef
   Russian dressing
2 slices tomato
   Shredded lettuce

Arrange chicken on bagel bottoms, then add corned beef folded in half. Cover with tomato slices and shredded lettuce. Spread tops with Russian dressing and cover sandwiches. *Makes 2 servings.*

Chicken Curry Bagel

The best way to get your palate used to curry is to use only a bit at a time. Each time you add more, taste to be sure it has the kick of flavor you like.

1 cup cooked chicken, diced
$\frac{1}{4}$ cup chopped peanuts
$\frac{1}{4}$ cup mayonnaise
$\frac{1}{4}$ teaspoon curry powder
4 sesame seed bagels, cut in half
4 lettuce leaves

Combine chicken and peanuts. Stir mayonnaise and curry powder together and mix through chicken. Spread chicken mixture on bagel bottoms. Cover with lettuce leaves and then close with bagel tops. *Makes 4 servings.*

Chopped Liver Bagel

Sure you can buy chopped chicken livers at your local deli, but first see how easy it is to make them yourself. This method poaches, rather than fries, the livers. It tastes better and it's better for you.

1 pound fresh chicken livers
1 onion, sliced thin
2 hard-cooked eggs
$\frac{1}{4}$ teaspoon salt
$\frac{1}{8}$ teaspoon pepper
8 bagels, cut in half
8 thick slices tomato

Place chicken livers and sliced onion rings in a large skillet. Barely cover the bottom of the skillet with water. Cover and simmer for 5 minutes, turning the livers several times and adding more water if necessary to prevent livers from sticking to pan. With a slotted spoon, remove livers and onion to a chopping bowl and chop until fine. Add eggs and chop until well blended. Add salt and pepper. Add a small amount of pan juices if necessary to hold the mixture together. Chill until ready to use. Spread chopped liver on all bagel halves. Place a tomato slice on each bagel bottom and cover with bagel tops. *Makes 8 servings.*

Note: Livers and onion may be sautéed in chicken fat if you prefer the traditional way.

Duckling Apple Bagel

Reheated duckling can taste pretty tired. Here's a way to wake up your taste buds by serving it cold and spicy.

4 bagels, cut in half
   Butter or margarine
8 slices cooked roast duckling
4 spiced apple rings
   (available in jars)
   Orange marmalade

Spread bagel bottoms with butter or margarine. Top with duckling slices, then add an apple ring on each bottom. Spread orange marmalade thinly on bagel tops and cover sandwiches. *Makes 4 servings.*

Egg on a Bagel

Baked Egg in a Bagel

Yes, a bagel can also be a baking dish—edible and with a neat appearance. Tuck a bit of corned beef, tongue, or bologna under the egg for a different taste.

2 bagels, cut in half
4 eggs
1 teaspoon finely chopped parsley
$\frac{1}{4}$ teaspoon salt
$\frac{1}{8}$ teaspoon white pepper

Tear out some of the soft interior of bagel halves and stuff it into center holes. Place, crust side down, on a baking sheet. Break 1 egg into each bagel cup. Sprinkle with parsley, salt, and pepper. Bake in a 350° F. oven for 20 minutes, or until set. *Makes 4 servings.*

Egg Florentine Bagel

It's best to trim the Swiss cheese to fit the top of the egg and not let it hang over the sides. Saves a melting mess and looks neater.

1 package (10-ounce) frozen spinach
$\frac{1}{4}$ teaspoon nutmeg
1 teaspoon grated onion
6 eggs
3 bagels, cut in half
6 slices Swiss cheese

Place spinach, nutmeg, and onion in a saucepan with a small amount of water. Cover and cook for 10 minutes, or until spinach is hot. Drain very well. Meanwhile, fry eggs. Spread a layer of spinach on each bagel bottom, then top with a fried egg. Add a slice of Swiss cheese and slip under the broiler until cheese begins to melt. Serve at once. *Makes 6 servings.*

Eggs 'n' Tomato Sauce Bagel

Poach the eggs in tomato sauce and spoon the extra sauce over the assembled egg on a bagel. Fast and fancy too!

1 tablespoon butter	$\frac{1}{4}$ teaspoon oregano
$\frac{1}{2}$ onion, sliced thin	4 eggs
1 can (8-ounce) tomato sauce	2 bagels, cut in half

Melt butter in a large skillet; sauté onion until limp. Add tomato sauce to skillet. When sauce is hot, stir in oregano and break eggs, one at a time, into the sauce, being careful to keep the eggs from touching one another. Cover skillet and lower heat. Cook for several minutes until whites are solidified (about 4 minutes). Spoon one cooked egg with sauce onto each bagel half. Top with remaining sauce. *Makes 4 servings.*

Egg McBagel

How can you improve on a chive and cheese omelet? Put it on a bagel, of course, and serve your breakfast all-in-one.

2 eggs	1 teaspoon chopped chives
1 tablespoon cold water	1 tablespoon grated Cheddar
1 tablespoon butter	cheese
$\frac{1}{8}$ teaspon salt	2 bagels, cut in half

Beat together eggs and water. Melt butter in a small skillet; pour in egg mixture and cook until some egg solidifies. Push solid egg to center of skillet to permit liquid egg to run to edges. Sprinkle with salt, chopped chives, and grated cheese. While eggs are still slightly moist and cheese is semi-melted, remove mixture from heat. Pile onto two bagel bottoms and cover with bagel tops. *Makes 2 servings.*

Eggs Benedict Bagel

Egg-poaching rings are sold in the housewares department of your local store if you want to take the risk out of making nicely shaped eggs. Merely set them in the skillet and break an egg into each ring.

$\frac{1}{2}$ pound fresh mushrooms
2 tablespoons butter
2 bagels, cut in half
4 eggs
1 tablespoon vinegar
1 cup Blender Hollandaise Sauce

Sauté mushrooms in butter until limp. Spoon onto bagel halves. Poach eggs by breaking them, one at a time, into a skillet of boiling water to which 1 tablespoon of vinegar has been added. Reduce heat and swirl whites of egg over yolk as it tends to wisp away. Cook 4 minutes. Remove with a slotted spoon and drain well. Place on mushrooms and cover with warm hollandaise sauce. Serve at once. *Makes 4 servings.*

Blender Hollandaise Sauce

There's no need to worry about curdling sauce when you use this foolproof method of making hollandaise in an electric blender. It emulsifies into a smooth lemony sauce.

$\frac{1}{4}$ pound butter   2 teaspoons lemon juice
2 egg yolks $\frac{1}{4}$ teaspoon salt

Melt butter in a small saucepan. Place egg yolks in an electric blender; add lemon juice and salt. Blend on high, then turn to low and add melted butter a little at a time. Turn blender off at the last drop. *Makes 1 cup sauce.*

Note: This sauce can be refrigerated for several days in a tightly covered jar.

Corned Beef Bagel Benedict

This is a rich and delicious offering. The hollandaise sauce can be made ahead and warmed up just before using.

2 bagels, cut in half
4 slices lean, cooked corned beef, cut in half
3 cups water
1 teaspoon vinegar
4 eggs
1 cup Blender Hollandaise Sauce
Dash paprika

Top each bagel half with corned beef; tuck edges under to conform to round shape of bagel. Pour water and vinegar into a skillet; bring to a boil. Carefully break each egg into the water, spooning wisps of solidifying egg white over the yolks. Try to keep each egg in a circular shape. Reduce heat and simmer several minutes until white has solidified and yolk is still soft (about 4 minutes). Remove eggs with a slotted spoon and place them on paper toweling to drain a moment. Carefully place each egg on the prepared corned beef on bagel. Spoon hollandaise sauce over eggs. Sprinkle lightly with paprika. Serve at once. *Makes 4 servings.*

Scrambled Pepper Bagel

Don't let the eggs overcook—remove them from the heat when the bottom of the mixture is solid but the top still runny. By the time you spoon them out of the pan, the eggs will be fluffy but not dry.

2 eggs
1 tablespoon cold water
$\frac{1}{2}$ green pepper, seeded and diced
$\frac{1}{2}$ small onion, diced
2 tablespoons butter
$\frac{1}{4}$ teaspoon salt
2 rye bagels, cut in half

Beat together eggs and water. Sauté pepper and onion in butter until limp. Pour egg mixture into skillet, swirling pepper and onion into mixture. Sprinkle with salt. Push solidifying egg to the center to permit liquid egg to run to edges. When cooked but still moist, remove mixture from heat. Pile onto two bagel bottoms and cover with bagel tops. *Makes 2 servings.*

Corned Beef Western Bagel

No need to add salt to the eggs as the corned beef has enough for both. Double up and serve open-face, if you desire.

2 tablespoons butter or margarine
1 onion, sliced thin
$\frac{1}{2}$ green pepper, seeded and diced
4 slices cooked corned beef, diced
4 eggs
4 bagels, cut in half

Melt butter in a skillet. Sauté onion and green pepper until limp. Add diced corned beef. Beat eggs and pour into skillet; scramble all together. Spoon onto bagel bottoms and cover with buttered bagel tops. *Makes 4 servings.*

Egg Foo Yong Bagel

Bagels are a versatile base for ethnic food. Here's the way to turn a bit of leftover cooked chicken and diced fresh vegetables into a Chinese omelet with a Jewish accent.

4 eggs
1 tablespoon cold water
1 cup finely diced chicken
½ cup fresh bean sprouts
1 scallion, diced fine
½ cup chopped celery

¼ teaspoon salt
¼ teaspoon soy sauce
   Cooking oil
4 sesame seed bagels, cut in half
   Shredded lettuce

Beat eggs lightly; add water. Add chicken, bean sprouts, scallion, and celery. Add salt and soy sauce. Heat a 6-inch skillet and brush lightly with oil. Pour ¼ of the mixture into the skillet and cook until lightly browned on one side, then turn and brown the other side. Repeat until 4 small omelets are made. Place omelets on bagel bottoms and cover with shredded lettuce. Cover sandwiches with bagel tops. *Makes 4 servings.*

Deviled-Egg Lox Bagel

It's the mustard that makes the mayonnaise "devilish" when you mix it through chopped egg. Amazing what a bit of spice can do.

4 sliced smoked salmon
4 bagels, cut in half
2 hard-cooked eggs, chopped
2 tablespoons mayonnaise
$\frac{1}{8}$ teaspoon dried mustard

Arrange smoked salmon over each bagel bottom. Combine mayonnaise and dry mustard; mix with chopped eggs. Spread a layer of egg mixture over smoked salmon. Cover with bagel tops. *Makes 4 servings.*

Egg Salad Bagel

Dill weed gives egg salad a piquant flavor; celery gives it crunch. When combined with tomato and green pepper, it makes a sandwich you'll want to munch.

4 hard-cooked eggs, coarsely chopped
2 tablespoons finely minced celery
2 tablespoons mayonnaise
1 teaspoon dried dill weed
$\frac{1}{4}$ teaspoon salt
4 poppy seed bagels, cut in half
4 thick slices tomato
4 thin slices green pepper, seeds removed
  Mayonnaise

Add celery, mayonnaise, dill weed, and salt to chopped eggs. Spread egg salad in a thick layer on bagel bottoms. Cover with tomato and pepper slices. Spread additional mayonnaise on bagel tops and cover sandwiches. *Makes 4 servings.*

Caviar Egg Bagel

No need to use Beluga's best caviar when a simple black variety will do. Pile chopped onion atop the caviar if that's your favorite duo and don't forget the dill weed that presses gently into the buttered top.

4 rye bagels, cut in half
$\frac{1}{2}$ cup black caviar
4 hard-cooked eggs, sliced thin
2 teaspoons dried dill weed
Softened butter

Spread bagel bottoms with black caviar. Arrange egg slices, overlapping slightly, in a circle over caviar. Sprinkle with dill weed. Spread butter on bagel tops and cover sandwiches. *Makes 4 servings.*

French Toasted Bagel

This French toast comes out extra soft if you allow the bagels to soak up the egg mixture for several minutes, instead of just dunking them to coat. Good with jelly too!

1 egg
$\frac{1}{4}$ cup milk
$\frac{1}{2}$ teaspoon vanilla extract
2 tablespoons butter
2 raisin bagels, cut in half
Whipped butter
Maple syrup

Beat together egg, milk, and vanilla. Melt 2 tablespoons butter in a large skillet. Dip bagel halves into the batter and then brown in the skillet, turning each over once. Serve with whipped butter and maple syrup. *Makes 2 servings.*

Salami Quiche Bagel

Here's a novel way to make individual quiches. Use a scooped-out bagel for each crust, fill, and bake. Green pepper, lox, or sliced mushrooms may be substituted for salami. Or dream up your own combination before pouring in the custard.

    4 bagels, cut in half
    ½ cup finely diced salami
    ½ cup coarsely diced Swiss cheese
    ¼ cup coarsely chopped onion
    2 eggs, beaten
    ⅔ cup dairy sour cream
    ½ teaspoon salt
    ½ teaspoon Worcestershire sauce

Tear excess bread out of bagel halves and flatten centers to form a shell. Arrange bagel shells on a baking pan. Combine salami, Swiss cheese, and onion; divide among the bagel shells. Beat eggs; add sour cream, salt, and Worcestershire sauce and beat well. Pour into bagel shells almost to the top. Bake in a 350° F. oven for 20 minutes, or until custard is lightly browned. *Makes 8 servings.*

Cheese on a Bagel

Grilled Cheese Tomato Bagel

Sometimes the simplest combinations have the most rewarding tastes. Don't forget the oregano if you want a pizza-like aroma.

8 slices processed American cheese
8 thin slices tomato
4 bagels, cut in half
1 teaspoon oregano

Arrange a slice of cheese topped with a slice of tomato on each bagel half. Sprinkle with oregano. Broil for several minutes, until cheese melts. *Makes 8 pieces.*

Pizza Bagel

This recipe makes quick do-it-yourself pizza that is only as far away as your freezer. What other snack could you have on the table in five minutes flat?

4 bagels, cut in half
1 can (8-ounce) tomato sauce
1 tablespoon grated Parmesan cheese
½ teaspoon dried oregano
1 cup shredded mozzarella cheese

Place bagel halves, cut side up, on a broiling pan. Combine tomato sauce, Parmesan cheese, and oregano; spoon over bagels. Top with shredded mozzarella cheese. Broil until cheese melts, about 4 minutes. Serve at once. *Makes 8 pieces.*

Variations: Add chopped onion, chopped green pepper, or sliced mushrooms to the shredded cheese topping.

Rarebit Bagel

Here's a simple cheese rarebit with a beer base. But there's nothing simple about the taste. It's great for a late snack or a late Sunday supper.

2 cups shredded Cheddar cheese
¼ teaspoon dry mustard
½ teaspoon Worcestershire sauce
1 egg, lightly beaten
¼ cup beer
3 bagels, cut in half

Heat cheese, mustard, and Worcestershire sauce in the top of a double boiler over simmering water, until cheese melts. Stir frequently. Add beaten egg to beer and add mixture gradually to cheese mixture. Cook, over water, until mixture is thick and smooth. Arrange a bagel half on each plate; spoon rarebit over bagels. *Makes 6 servings.*

Triple Cheese Bagel

How cheesey can you get? In this recipe three cheeses complement one another—and the sweet red onion sends it home.

4 rye bagels, cut in half
1 package (3-ounce) cream cheese
4 slices Swiss cheese
4 slices Muenster cheese
4 thin slices red onion

Spread all bagel halves with cream cheese. On bagel bottoms, place Swiss cheese and Muenster cheese, then add a slice of onion to each. Cover with bagel tops. *Makes 4 servings.*

Blue Cheese Nut Bagel

*If you fancy blue cheese you'll really go for this brandy-laced nut and raisin combo.
Perfect open-face accompaniment to a luncheon salad.*

8 ounces blue cheese	¼ cup chopped walnuts
1 tablespoon brandy	Softened butter
2 tablespoons raisins	4 bagels, cut in half

Combine blue cheese, brandy, raisins, and walnuts into a spreadable
consistency. Spread butter on bagel halves, then cover with blue cheese mixture.
Serve open-face with a topping of additional chopped walnuts, or put halves
together and serve as sandwiches. *Makes 4 servings.*

Cheese Radish Bagel

*This was inspired by eastern European farm sandwiches of
dark bread and butter with sliced root vegetables and cheese.
On a bagel, it's a daintier offering—but it's just as*

4 rye bagels, cut in half
   Softened butter
8 slices Muenster cheese
4 large radishes, sliced paper thin

Spread bagel halves with butter. Arrange two slices of cheese on each bagel
bottom. Arrange a circlet of overlapping radish slices over cheese. Cover with
bagel tops. *Makes 6 servings.*

Broiled Mushroom Cheese Bagel

Tuck the stick-out corners of cheese under to conform to the bagel circle. It looks better and prevents dripping.

    8 slices Swiss cheese
    4 bagels, cut in half
    1 cup sliced fresh mushrooms
    1 tablespoon grated Parmesan cheese

Fold each slice of cheese in half and place on bagel halves. Arrange sliced mushrooms over cheese. Sprinkle with grated Parmesan cheese. Broil until Swiss cheese melts. *Makes 8 pieces.*

Cream Cheese and Olive Bagel

Here's a dandy sandwich for brown-baggers. A bit of bologna under the tomato would give it an extra protein punch.

    1 package (8-ounce) cream cheese
    6 pimiento-stuffed green olives, chopped
    ¼ teaspoon dried dill weed
    1 tablespoon dairy sour cream
    4 bagels, cut in half
    4 slices tomato

Mash together cream cheese, olives, dill weed, and sour cream. Spread mixture on all bagel halves. Place tomato slices on bagel bottoms. Cover with bagel tops. *Makes 4 servings.*

Health Cheese Bagel

There's a mouthful of fluffy goodness in every bite.
For variety, add some freshly sprouted
mung beans or finely diced celery.

    1 package (8-ounce) cream cheese
    ¼ cup shredded carrots
    ¼ cup chopped walnuts
    ¼ cup seedless raisins
    1 tablespoon dairy sour cream
    4 rye bagels, cut in half

Combine cream cheese, carrots, walnuts, raisins, and sour cream; mix well. Spread on bagel bottoms in a thick layer. Cover with bagel tops. *Makes 4 servings.*

Pineapple Cheese Bagel

A variation of this combination would be to mix crushed pineapple right into the cheese mixture. Either way, sweet onion gives it a zesty boost.

    1 package (8-ounce) cream cheese
    1 tablespoon dairy sour cream
    ½ teaspoon dried dill weed
    4 bagels, cut in half
    4 canned pineapple rings, drained well
    4 thin slices sweet onion

Mash together cream cheese, sour cream, and dill weed until soft and fluffy. Spread mixture on bagel halves. Place pineapple rings on bottom halves, then add onion slices. Cover with top halves. *Makes 4 servings.*

Spinach Cheese Bagel

Be sure to drain the spinach well before adding to the cheese. Chopped scallions would liven up the flavor too!

$\frac{1}{2}$ cup cottage cheese
$\frac{1}{2}$ cup cold cooked chopped spinach, drained well
$\frac{1}{2}$ teaspoon chopped parsley
$\frac{1}{8}$ teaspoon nutmeg
4 bagels, cut in half

Combine cheese, spinach, parsley, and nutmeg. Spread mixture over bagel bottoms. Cover with bagel tops. *Makes 4 servings.*

Bagel Danish

You don't have to be a Danish baker to turn a bagel into a Danish treat. Increase the cinnamon if that flavor gives you a kick.

2 bagels, cut in half
1 cup cottage cheese
1 teaspoon vanilla extract
$\frac{1}{4}$ cup seedless raisins
2 teaspoons soft brown sugar
$\frac{1}{4}$ teaspoon cinnamon

Arrange bagel halves in a baking dish. Combine cottage cheese, vanilla, and raisins. Spread mixture on each bagel half. Sprinkle with brown sugar and cinnamon. Broil for a moment to heat through. *Makes 4 servings.*

Diet Bagel

If you have a slick knife that will slice the bagel thinner, go to it. Toast each slice if you want, and skinny down the enjoyable way.

1 bagel, cut in 6 thin rounds
6 thick slices tomato
¾ cup low-fat (1%) cottage cheese
6 thin circles green pepper
2 tablespoons chopped chives
   Paprika

On each bagel slice, place a tomato slice, then 2 tablespoons cottage cheese. Add a green pepper ring to each bagel slice. Sprinkle with chives and paprika. *Makes 6 servings.*

Hawaiian Bagel

Here's a way to give everyday cottage cheese a special toothsomeness. Add a dash of cinnamon if you like a spicy tang.

½ cup cottage cheese
2 tablespoons canned crushed
   pineapple, drained
2 bagels, cut in half
2 tablespoons coconut flakes
2 teaspoons soft brown sugar

Combine cottage cheese and crushed pineapple. Spread mixture on bagel halves. Sprinkle with coconut flakes and brown sugar. Broil for several minutes, until coconut is lightly browned. *Makes 4 pieces.*

Vegetables on a Bagel

Cucumber Tomato Bagel

When you're in the mood to keep it simple, this is a refreshing combination to consider. The thinner the cucumber, the more delectable the taste.

4 bagels, cut in half
1 cucumber, sliced thin
4 slices tomato
4 teaspoons chopped chives
   Softened butter

On each bagel bottom arrange a circlet of overlapping cucumber slices. Top with tomato slices. Sprinkle tomato with chopped chives. Spread butter over bagel tops and cover sandwiches. *Makes 4 servings.*

Potato Pancake Bagel

Don't grate the potatoes in advance or they will turn black and taste gritty. Drop them into a bowl of salty water as you peel, to keep them white until you are ready to grate.

2 pounds potatoes, pared
2 onions
1 egg, slightly beaten
2 tablespoons flour
$\frac{1}{2}$ teaspoon salt
$\frac{1}{4}$ teaspoon pepper
1 cup peanut oil
6 raisin bagels, cut in half
$\frac{1}{2}$ cup applesauce

Grate potatoes and onions into a deep bowl. Add egg, flour, salt, and pepper; mix well. Heat peanut oil in a large skillet. Drop large spoonfuls of mixture into the hot oil and fry until browned on one side, then turn and brown the other side. Drain on paper toweling. Place a potato pancake on each bagel bottom, spread with applesauce, and top with a second pancake. Cover with bagel tops. *Makes 6 servings.*

Ratatouille Cheese Bagel

Ratatouille is a French vegetable stew. It makes a fascinating base for a grilled cheese sandwich.

$\frac{1}{4}$ cup olive oil
1 large onion, sliced
1 garlic clove, minced
1 eggplant, peeled and diced
1 zucchini, cut in $\frac{1}{4}$-inch slices
3 tomatoes, cut in wedges
2 green peppers, seeded
  and cut in squares

$\frac{1}{2}$ teaspoon salt
$\frac{1}{4}$ teaspoon oregano
$\frac{1}{8}$ teaspoon pepper
4 bagels, cut in half
8 slices processed
  American cheese

Heat oil in a heavy skillet. Sauté onion and garlic until onion is golden. Add eggplant, zucchini, tomatoes, and green peppers. Add salt, oregano, and pepper. Cover and simmer for 20 minutes, stirring occasionally. Spoon mixture onto bagel halves. Top each half with a slice of cheese. Broil for a few minutes, until cheese melts. Serve at once. *Makes 8 servings.*

Grilled Asparagus Bagel

Steam the asparagus only until tender. If you overcook them, the flavor and texture are not as fine. Some children call melted Gruyère "bubble-gum cheese."

4 bagels, cut in half
  Softened Butter
$\frac{1}{2}$ pound fresh thin asparagus, steamed
8 slices Gruyère cheese

Spread all bagel halves with butter. Cut cooked asparagus into 3-inch segments. Lay asparagus side by side on each bagel half. Top with Gruyère cheese. Slip under the broiler until cheese melts. Serve at once. *Makes 8 servings.*

Corn Fritter Bagel

Old-fashioned corn fritters take on new life as a bagel filling. Red spiced apple rings are available in jars at your supermarket. They have holes, just like the bagels!

2 eggs, separated
1 cup canned or cooked
   kernel corn, drained
$\frac{1}{2}$ teaspoon salt
$\frac{1}{4}$ teaspoon Tabasco sauce

3 tablespoons flour
   Fat for deep frying
4 egg bagels, cut in half
4 spiced apple rings
   Tartar sauce

Beat egg yolks until light. Mix in corn, salt, Tabasco sauce, and flour. Beat egg whites until stiff but not dry; fold into corn mixture. Drop by serving spoon into skillet of hot fat, making 4 large fritters. When fritters are browned on one side, turn and brown the other side. Drain. Place fritters on bagel bottoms. Cover with apple rings. Spread bagel tops with tartar sauce and cover sandwiches. *Makes 4 servings.*

Mock Chopped Liver Bagel

This is a vegetable mixture that resembles chopped chicken livers in texture and taste. The surprise binder is peanut butter.

2 cups cooked string beans, fresh or canned	$\frac{1}{2}$ teaspoon salt
2 hard-cooked eggs	$\frac{1}{4}$ teaspoon pepper
1 onion, sliced	4 bagels, cut in half
1 tablespoon chicken fat	4 slices tomato
1 tablespoon peanut butter	$\frac{1}{4}$ cup mayonnaise
	$\frac{1}{8}$ teaspoon dried tarragon

Drain string beans and place in chopping bowl. Add peeled hard-cooked eggs. Sauté onion in chicken fat until golden; add to the chopping bowl. Chop all very fine. Add peanut butter. Season with salt and pepper. Spread bagel bottoms with a thick layer of mixture. Top with tomato. Combine mayonnaise and tarragon; spread on bagel tops and cover sandwiches. *Makes 4 servings.*

Chopped Eggplant Bagel

Eggplant has a versatility all its own. Here it is used as a spread with a lovely balance of lemon juice and sugar to give a subtle flavor.

1 medium eggplant	1 teaspoon sugar
1 small onion, diced	1 tablespoon peanut oil
2 tablespoons lemon juice	6 rye bagels, cut in half
$\frac{3}{4}$ teaspoon salt	6 pieces lettuce
$\frac{1}{4}$ teaspoon pepper	Softened butter

Bake the whole eggplant, uncovered, in a 350° F. oven until the skin turns dark brown and is wrinkled. Remove from oven, cut the skin away, and cut eggplant into large pieces. Place eggplant, onion, lemon juice, salt, pepper, and sugar into a chopping bowl. Chop very fine. Add oil and mix well. Spread bagel bottoms with mixture. Cover with lettuce. Spread tops with butter and cover sandwiches. *Makes 6 servings.*

Creamed Mushrooms on Bagel

Use a bagel half as a base for this creamy mushroom dish. Add cut-up chicken livers if you want a meal-in-one.

1 pound fresh mushrooms
2 tablespoons butter
$\frac{1}{4}$ teaspoon salt
1 teaspoon lemon juice
1 cup heavy cream
2 egg bagels, cut in half

Wash, dry, and slice mushrooms and stems. Sauté in butter until soft. Add salt and lemon juice. Stir in cream and cook, stirring occasionally, for about 3 minutes. Place a bagel half on each plate and cover with hot creamed mushrooms. *Makes 4 servings.*

Spinach Salad Bagel

Put a spinach salad on a bagel for a healthy lunch or snack. If you prepared it ahead of time, squeeze some lemon juice on the sliced mushrooms to keep them snowy white.

2 pumpernickel bagels, cut in half
2 tablespoons mayonnaise
$\frac{1}{2}$ teaspoon prepared mustard
1 hard-cooked egg, sliced into rings
$\frac{1}{4}$ cup sliced fresh mushrooms
6 fresh spinach leaves, trimmed

Spread bagel bottoms with a mixture of mayonnaise and mustard. Top with egg slices, then with a layer of mushroom slices, and finally with spinach leaves. Spread remaining mayonnaise mixture on bagel tops and cover sandwiches. *Makes 2 servings.*

Health Salad Bagel

Sprout your own mung bean seeds in just a few days, then crisp them in the refrigerator by soaking them in cold water. Makes a crunchy and nutritious topping.

4 pumpernickel bagels, cut in half	1 grated raw carrot
½ cup cottage cheese	4 thick slices tomato
1 tablespoon chopped fresh parsley	Bean sprouts
	Russian dressing

Spread mixture of cottage cheese, parsley, and carrot on bagel bottoms. Add tomato slices and a topping of bean sprouts. Spread bagel tops with Russian dressing and cover sandwiches. *Makes 4 servings.*

Falafel Bagel

Instead of tiny chick-pea balls, cooked and stuffed into Middle Eastern pita bread, here the mixture is cooked into a flat patty. Just the right size for a bagel!

8 ounces raw chick peas, soaked overnight	¼ teaspoon pepper
¼ cup bulghur wheat, soaked 1 hour	1 egg, beaten slightly
3 tablespoons flour	Fat for deep frying
1 clove garlic	4 bagels, cut in half
½ teaspoon salt	1 tablespoon chopped parsley
½ teaspoon cumin powder	1 tablespoon sesame seeds
	Shredded lettuce

Drain chick peas and bulghur wheat well. Place in a chopping bowl or food processor; add flour, garlic, salt, cumin, and pepper. Chop fine. Add beaten egg and mix well. Form into four patties. Fry in hot, deep fat until browned on both sides. Drain. Place each patty on a bagel bottom. Sprinkle with parsley and sesame seeds, then add shredded lettuce. Cover with bagel tops. *Makes 4 servings.*

Waldorf Salad Bagel

This is a refreshing combination of flavors and textures.
The raisin bagel gives it another dimension.

- 1 cup diced apple, seeds removed
- 2 tablespoons lemon juice
- ½ cup diced celery
- ½ cup broken walnuts
- ¼ cup mayonnaise
- 4 raisin bagels, cut in half
- Shredded lettuce
- Mayonnaise

Combine diced apple and lemon juice, coating apples well to prevent them from turning brown. Add celery, walnuts, and mayonnaise. Spread mixture thickly on bagel bottoms, then add shredded lettuce. Spread additional mayonnaise on bagel tops, if desired, and cover sandwiches. *Makes 4 servings.*

Banana Peanut Butter Bagel

Here's a yummy lunch or snack idea that packs a wallop of protein. What seems like a treat is really a nutritious combination.

- 2 raisin bagels, cut in half
- Chunky peanut butter
- Strawberry jam
- 1 banana, sliced

Spread bagel bottoms thickly with chunky peanut butter. Spread bagel tops thickly with strawberry jam. Arrange banana slices over peanut butter and cover with bagel tops. *Makes 2 servings.*

Hors d' Oeuvre Bagels

Antipasto Bagel

Caponata is a delicious Italian eggplant creation, sometimes containing bits of stuffed olives. It's a toothsome addition to any antipasto selection.

> 4 bagels, cut in half
> 1 can (4-ounce) caponata
> 1 can (7-ounce) tuna fish, drained
> 1 can (2-ounce) anchovies, flat style
> 4 whole pimientos
> ¼ cup mayonnaise
> 1 teaspoon capers

Spread bagel bottoms with caponata. Break tuna fish into small pieces with a fork; arrange over caponata. Top with several anchovies; add a pimiento to each. Combine mayonnaise and capers; spread on bagel tops and cover sandwiches. *Makes 4 servings.*

Hors d'Oeuvre Wedge Bagel

When is cream cheese and lox on a bagel not really a bagel? When it's a bite-size portion! Prepare and pile up these wedges for happy fingers to pick during the cocktail hour.

> 1 package (3-ounce) cream
>   cheese with chives
> 1 tablespoon dairy sour cream
>
> 6 bagels, cut in half
> ¼ pound thinly sliced lox

Mash together cheese and sour cream until soft and fluffy. Spread on bagel halves. Add a layer of lox to bagel bottoms and cover with prepared top halves. Cut each bagel sandwich into 6 equal parts. Place wedges in a serving bowl (preferably a glass snifter-shaped bowl) and serve as cocktail snacks. *Makes 3 dozen.*

Salami Pizza Bagel

If you plan to use an electric food processor instead of a food grinder for this, place all ingredients including the tomato paste into the processor. It takes only a moment to make incredible tastes.

> 1 pound salami, sliced
> ½ pound processed American cheese, sliced
> 1 green pepper, seeded and cut up
> 1 can (6-ounce) tomato paste
> 1 teaspoon oregano
> 12 bagelettes, cut in half

Put salami, cheese, and green pepper through a food grinder. Add tomato paste and oregano. Spread mixture on halves of bagelettes. Bake in a hot 450° F. oven for 15 minutes. Serve hot. *Makes 2 dozen.*

Pecan Cheese Bagel

Pick a pretty dish to show off this tongue-tingling cheese spread. Pecans turn it into something else!

> 1 package (3-ounce) cream cheese
> ½ cup grated Cheddar cheese
> ½ cup sieved cottage cheese
> 1 tablespoon grated orange rind
> 1 teaspoon Grand Marnier liqueur
> ¼ cup chopped pecans
> ¼ cup pecan halves
> 12 bagelettes, cut in half

Mash cheeses together until smooth. Add orange rind, Grand Marnier, and chopped pecans; mix well. Turn into a serving dish and arrange pecan halves over top of mixture. Surround with bagelette halves for spreading. *Makes 2 dozen.*

Salmon Canapé Bagel

Garnish these canapés the Danish way, making a food picture of onion, parsley, and capers on a background of pale pink lox. Twist the lemon sliver and tuck it to the side for both flair and flavor.

6 bagelettes, cut in half
Softened sweet butter
1/2 pound thinly sliced smoked salmon
1/4 cup finely chopped sweet onion
1/4 cup finely chopped fresh parsley
1/4 cup capers, drained
24 paper-thin half lemon slices

Cut bagelette halves horizontally in half again, making 4 thin circles of each half. Spread one side of each piece with softened butter. Top with piece of smoked salmon. Garnish each piece with a sprinkling of onion, fresh parsley, capers, and a sliver of lemon. *Makes 2 dozen.*

Sherried Cheese Bagel

This cheese spread is too delectable for a mundane cracker. Spread it on half a bagelette and munch with glee.

1/2 pound Cheddar cheese, grated
1/4 pound blue cheese, crumbled
1 package (3-ounce) cream cheese
1/4 cup dry sherry
1/2 teaspoon Worcestershire sauce
1/2 teaspoon paprika
1/2 teaspoon onion powder
1/4 teaspoon garlic powder
Dash cayenne pepper
12 bagelettes, cut in half

Have cheeses at room temperature. In a bowl, blend cheeses well with a fork or electric beater. Gradually beat in sherry and Worcestershire sauce. Add paprika, onion powder, garlic powder, and cayenne pepper. Beat until creamy. Pack into a lightly oiled mold. Store, covered, in the refrigerator. Unmold on a bed of lettuce and surround with bagelette halves for spreading. *Makes about 2 cups of spread.*

Bagel Fondue

Keep stirring the fondue in a figure-eight motion as you dunk a bagel into the melted mixture. Keep the heat low, and when all is done, divide the hardened disc at the bottom for the last of the happy dunkers.

1 garlic clove, cut
1 cup dry white wine
8 ounces Gruyère cheese, cubed
2 tablespoons Kirsch
¼ teaspoon pepper
¼ teaspoon nutmeg
4 bagels, cut in half

Rub interior of fondue pot with cut garlic clove; discard. Pour in wine, cubed cheese, and Kirsch. Stir over low heat until cheese is melted and smooth. Add pepper and nutmeg. Keep warm over a candle warmer or other device to provide low heat. Cut each bagel half into 6 chunks. Place a bagel chunk on the end of a long fondue fork and dunk it in the fondue pot, coating the chunk well.
Makes 8 servings.

Index

A

Anchovy Caper Bagel, 39
Antipasto Bagel, 90
Apricot Frank Bagel, 49

B

Bagelburger, 49
Bagel Danish, 79
Bagel Divan, 60
Bagel Fondue, 93
Bagel Grinder, 44
Baked Egg in a Bagel, 64
Banana Peanut Butter Bagel, 88
Beet 'n' Herring Bagel, 40
Blender Hollandaise Sauce, 66
Blue Cheese Nut Bagel, 76
Bologna Bagel, 45
Bologna Stack Bagel, 45
Broiled Mushroom Cheese Bagel, 77

C

Caviar Egg Bagel, 71
Cheese Radish Bagel, 76
Chicken à la King Bagel, 59
Chicken Cheese Bagel, 58
Chicken Curry Bagel, 61
Chicken Walnut Salad Bagel, 58
Chili Con Carne Bagel, 51
Chopped Eggplant Bagel, 85
Chopped Herring Bagel, 40
Chopped Liver Bagel, 62

Chopped Liver Turkey Bagel, 60
Club Bagel, 61
Corned Beef Bagel Benedict, 67
Corned Beef 'n' Cabbage Salad Bagel, 42
Corned Beef Western Bagel, 68
Corn Fritter Bagel, 84
Cream Cheese and Olive Bagel, 77
Creamed Mushrooms on Bagel, 86
Cucumber Tomato Bagel, 82

D

Deviled-Egg Lox Bagel, 70
Diet Bagel, 80
Duckling Apple Bagel, 62

E

Egg Florentine Bagel, 64
Egg Foo Yong Bagel, 69
Egg McBagel, 65
Egg Salad Bagel, 70
Eggs Benedict Bagel, 66
Eggs 'n' Tomato Sauce Bagel, 65

F

Falafel Bagel, 87
Fishburger Bagel, 32
Fish Salad Bagel, 30
Fish Stick Bagel, 32
Frankfurter Bagel, 48
French Onion Steak Bagel, 50
French Toasted Bagel, 71

G

Gefilte Fish Bagel, 33
Giant Sloppy Joe Bagel, 48
Grilled Asparagus Bagel, 83
Grilled Cheese Tomato Bagel, 74
Grilled Tuna Bagel, 33

H

Hash on a Bagel, 50
Hawaiian Bagel, 80
Health Cheese Bagel, 78
Health Salad Bagel, 87
Hero Bagel, 43
Hobo Bagel, 46
Homemade Bagels, 24
Hors d'Oeuvre Wedge Bagel, 90
Hot Pastrami Bagel, 42

L

Lamb Cucumber Bagel, 54
Lox and Cream Cheese Bagel, 26
Lox Fin Bagel, 28
Lox Spread Bagel, 26

M

Mackerel Cheese Bagel, 38
Meatball Bagel, 47
Melted Swiss Tongue Bagel, 44
Mock Chopped Liver Bagel, 85

N

Nova Bagel Soufflé, 27

P

Pecan Cheese Bagel, 91
Pineapple Cheese Bagel, 78
Pizza Bagel, 74
Potato Pancake Bagel, 82

R

Rarebit Bagel, 75
Ratatouille Cheese Bagel, 73
Red Caviar Bagel, 28
Reuben Bagel, 43
Roast Beef Bagel, 52

S

Salami Pizza Bagel, 91
Salami Quiche Bagel, 72
Salmon Canapé Bagel, 92
Salmon Cheese Bagel, 36
Sardine Bagel, 39
Scrambled Pepper Bagel, 68
Sherried Cheese Bagel, 92
Sliced Chicken Bagel, 59
Smoked Sablefish Bagel, 30
Spinach Cheese Bagel, 79
Spinach Salad Bagel, 86
Sturgeon Bagel, 29
Swiss Nova Bagel, 27

T

Taco Bagel, 51
Tempura Bagel, 31
Tomato Herring Bagel, 38
Tomato Sardine Bagel, 37
Triple Cheese Bagel, 75
Tuna Avocado Bagel, 35
Tuna Cheese Bagel, 35
Tuna Chutney Bagel, 34
Tuna Pepper Bagel, 34
Tuna Pineapple Bagel, 36
Turkey Cranberry Bagel, 57

Turkey Dagwood Bagel, 57
Turkey in Horseradish Sauce Bagel, 56

V

Veal and Peppers Bagel, 53
Veal and Red Cabbage Bagel, 53

W

Waldorf Salad Bagel, 88
Whitefish Cheese Bagel, 29
Wimpy Bagel, 47